CONSTITUTION
for the
HOUSE OF GOD

DR. MARK DUPLANTIS

CREATION HOUSE
A STRANG COMPANY

THE CONSTITUTION FOR THE HOUSE OF GOD
by Dr. Mark Duplantis
Published by Creation House
A Strang Company
600 Rinehart Road
Lake Mary, Florida 32746
www.creationhouse.com

Unless otherwise noted, all Scripture quotations are from the King James version of the Bible.

Cover design by Terry Clifton

Library of Congress Control Number:
2006926082
International Standard Book Number:
1-59979-016-5

First Edition

06 07 08 09 10 — 9 8 7 6 5 4 3 2 1
Printed in the United States of America

I would like to dedicate this book to:

- My earthly father, Reverend Paul Duplantis, who is eighty-three years young at the time of this book's publication. He is still preaching the gospel and has impacted my life greatly with it.

- My wife, Helen, who, after thirty-three years of marriage, continues to allow God to condition her to the calling that He has placed on my life.

- To my three children, Mark Jr., Leslie, and Jesse, and my six grandchildren, Dylan, Tanner, Leah, Emily, Katherine, and Kelly, who all have a special place in my heart.

Thank You, God, for being God in my life. I am forever grateful.

Acknowledgments

Many thanks to some of my best friends in the ministry, Don and Kathy Channell, who inspired me in writing and preaching the message about the constitution for the house of God all over the world. They have believed in Helen and me from the first time we met. God bless them both!

CONTENTS

INTRODUCTION

*If we are to serve as ambassadors
of the kingdom of God, we must be
familiar with the constitution He has
given us in His Word.*

The Bible records many prayers for our spiritual instruction and growth. Perhaps the most well known prayer is the Lord's Prayer, which Jesus taught His disciples in Matthew 6:9–13. Another prayer that has touched the lives of many people is the prayer of Jabez. Although it is tucked away in the genealogy of the clans of Judah in 1 Chronicles 4:9–10, it has brought great blessing to many people through Bruce Wilkinson's book *The Prayer of Jabez.*

This book, *The Constitution of the House of God,* is based on another significant prayer—King Solomon's prayer of dedication for the temple. Found in 2 Chronicles 6:12–42, this prayer is God's constitution for the church. God accepted everything Solomon prayed in these verses; He did not oppose any of it. And He showed this by appearing in all His glory (2 Chron. 7:1–2). Later, in 2 Chronicles 7:12–16, God spoke to Solomon personally at night and further expressed His blessing by saying (author's paraphrase), "All that you have prayed, all that you have decreed, all you have declared will be my law. It will be My constitution for every church."

It is important that we understand the background for Solomon's prayer of dedication. His father, King David, had wanted to build a temple, and God commended this desire. However, God told David that he was not the one to build a house for Him because he was a warrior and had shed blood. Instead, his son Solomon would build the temple (1 Chron. 28:2–6; 2 Chron. 6:7–9). Even though David was not permitted to build a house for God, he supplied material for it. (1 Chron. 29:1–9). He said, "I might not be able to build the temple myself, but I can sow into it."

God blessed the fruit of David's gifts and Solomon's construction work. In 2 Chronicles 5, after the temple was completed, the priests brought the ark of the covenant and all the sacred furnishings into the house. The glory of God filled the temple, and the priests were not able to stand and minister. After giving praise to God in a brief address to the people (2 Chron. 6:1–11), Solomon offered his prayer of dedication for the temple. The result, in chapter 7, was that God's glory filled the temple again, and the priests were not able to enter it.

When we go to a church dedication, we often hear a message from 2 Chronicles 7. This is understandable because the gathering of God's people as the church represents the House of God. However, we hardly ever hear anyone preach on Solomon's prayer in 2 Chronicles 6. This book will show, verse by verse, the tenets that form God's constitution for the church today.

THE IMPORTANCE OF THE CONSTITUTION

When Solomon dedicated the temple, his prayer reflected all that God wants His House to be. It became the constitution of the House of God from the time Solomon prayed it until the very day in which we live. Nothing is to be added to it or taken away from it, and it is vital that we study it.

Constitution means structure, the basic laws of government. The structure of the church is based on the Person of Jesus Christ, the chief cornerstone (Eph. 2:20). Seven hundred years before Christ, Isaiah described Him prophetically as a Son who was to be given and said that the government would be upon His shoulders (Isa. 9:6).

God has also provided structure for the church through the written constitution He gave us in Solomon's dedication prayer. We need this structure

3

because it gives us a plan for the church to follow. If we neglect it or rebel against it, we have looseness and lawlessness. It is imperative, therefore, that we obey it.

Everybody lives by a constitution. Just as we who are United States citizens live under our nation's constitution, we in the church are to live according to the constitution God has given us. However, as I travel all over America, I am saddened to learn that many of God's people really don't know the constitution of the house of God. A person can go to seven different churches and each one will have different beliefs. It seems that churches care more about their ideas and opinions than the constitution that God ordained for the House of God.

I can go to any Wal-Mart in the United States and everything is structured the same. Wherever I travel, I can walk into a Wal-Mart and feel like I am at the one by my house. The same is true of Home Depot and many other chain stores. But when I go to church, I do not know what to expect, even though the government was put on the shoulders of Jesus.

Think about that for a moment. Something went wrong somewhere. We do not know what a church believes until we go and sit there awhile. Although God ordained the constitution of the house of God for every church, we have failed to obey it.

VITAL TRUTH
FOR EVERY CHURCH

I believe in the constitution of the house of God. In fact, if I pastor a church again, I am going to put that statement on a big plaque and place it in a prominent place in the church. Sad to say, many Christians do not know what this constitution is. If we did, we would not have so much disagreement and fighting among ourselves. We would be promoting unity rather than division.

The constitution of the house of God presents structure of the government He has ordained for us, and it needs to hold a central place in every church in America. He wants us to follow it, and we must be careful that we do not try to change it from His way to our way. Instead, we are called to practice its principles so people who pass by the church or step inside will see the glory of God revealed in us.

After we dedicate a church and the memory of the ceremony and celebration fades, we tend to forget that God has placed us in the community to reflect Christ and project His image to those around us. However, the Bible reminds us that we are ambassadors for Christ, representatives of the kingdom of God (2 Cor. 5:20). If we are to serve as ambassadors of the kingdom of God, we must be familiar with the constitution He has given us in His Word.

In the following pages we will discuss vital truth

for the church. We will examine 2 Chronicles 6:12–42, verse by verse, to find the nuggets that form the constitution of the house of God. It will be a study that is not only informative, but also an important, formative resource for the life and ministry of the church.

*And he stood before the altar of the Lord
in the presence of all the congregation of
Israel, and spread forth his hands: For
Solomon had made a brasen scaffold, of
five cubits long, and five cubits broad, and
three cubits high, and had set it in the midst
of the court: and upon it he stood, and
kneeled down upon his knees before all the
congregation of Israel, and spread forth his
hands toward heaven.*

—2 CHRONICLES 6:12–13

A POSTURE OF SURRENDER

Every church should be a
body of people who are in covenant
with God, are right with Him, and
show mercy to others.

A s we begin our study of Solomon's prayer, we see him standing on a platform. There he is, holding his hands out to God in an expression of surrender. But he does not remain in an upright position. Something happens in his heart, and, in the sight of all Israel, he kneels down before God.

Solomon may be the king of Israel, but he understands that God—the Creator and the very God of Israel—is worthy of his wholehearted worship. In a physical act of total surrender to God, he prepares to offer a prayer that becomes the constitution of the house of God, the church. Although it is a prayer of dedication for the temple, it reveals the structure, the basic law of government, for every church.

A House That Keeps
Covenant and Shows Mercy

And said, O Lord God of Israel, there is no
God like thee in the heaven, nor in the earth;
which keepest covenant, and showest mercy
unto thy servants, that walk before thee with
all their hearts.

—2 Chronicles 6:14

Solomon is down on his knees in humility before
God, and his hands are lifted up in surrender to
God. In this posture, he begins his prayer by saying
that the house of God is a place that keeps covenant.
Think about that. The church must keep covenant.

The permanent nature of a covenant is illus-
trated by the way two men made a covenant in the
old days. Each of them carried a pouch of salt, and
each one would take a pinch of salt from his pouch
and put it in the pouch of the other. The only way
either man could break covenant was to go back and
remove the grains of salt he had put in the pouch of
the other man. This, of course, was impossible.

If we understand the meaning of covenant, we
will not entertain doubts about God's care for us.
And we will take seriously the importance of mak-
ing the church a place where people can come and
know that we keep covenant with God.

Solomon also said the house of God is a place that
shows mercy. It is to be a place with people whose
hearts are right with God. But we see churches that

push their tenets of faith—what they believe—and break out the bylaws of their nonprofit organizations. While those things have their proper place, we are called to honor the constitution of the house of God.

Every church should be a body of people who are in covenant with God, are right with Him, and show mercy to others. Solomon is praying for this in the house of God, and God accepts his prayer.

Thou which has kept with thy servant David my father that which thou hast promised him; and spakest with thy mouth, and hast fulfilled it with thine hand, as it is this day. Now therefore, O LORD God of Israel, keep with thy servant David my father that which thou hast promised him, saying, There shall not fail thee a man in my sight to sit upon the throne of Israel; yet so that thy children take heed to their way to walk in my law, as thou hast walked before me. Now then, O LORD God of Israel, let thy word be verified, which thou hast spoken unto thy servant David.

—2 CHRONICLES 6:15–17

The Promises of an Unlimited God

*We must declare in word and
practice the truth that God is not
limited in the church.*

In these verses, Solomon says that the house of
God is to be a place blessed with God's generational promises. The church is not only a people
who keep covenant, show mercy, and have hearts
that are right with God. It is also a place where God
gives promises for the next generation. Our children
and our children's children will be able to come and
be in covenant with God and see the mercy of God.
They are promised a house of God with people who
have a right heart to worship and magnify God.

We do not hear very many people talk about the
church like that today. It is because they have not
read the constitution of the house of God. I have
not read China's constitution. But if I go there, I

need to be familiar with it so I know what should happen there.

Yes, the house of God is going to be a place where generational promises come to pass. Isn't that good? The same promises that God has given us are also for our children and our children's children, to a thousand generations. (See Deut. 7:9; Ps. 105:6–10; Rom. 4; 9:8; Gal. 4:28.) We can invest our time, energy, and money in the house of God because our labor will not be in vain for future generations. When we go to church, it is not just a place where we meet with other Christians for a couple hours. No, it is a place where the next generation is guaranteed promises. And that is something to shout about!

A HOUSE THAT DOES NOT LIMIT GOD

> But will God in very deed dwell with men on the earth? Behold, heaven and the heaven of heavens cannot contain thee; how much less this house which I have built! Have respect therefore to the prayer of thy servant, and to his supplication, O LORD my God, to harken unto the cry and the prayer which thy servant prayeth before thee.
>
> —2 CHRONICLES 6:18–19

As Solomon kneels in humility before God, he recognizes that the temple does not limit God. We need to understand this. You see, when we come to church we want to limit God. But God accepted Solomon's prayer when he said, "Lord God, this house cannot even contain Thee."

God has infinite, limitless power. Do not come into the house of God and limit Him by saying that He cannot heal your sickness and disease. Do not doubt His ability to restore broken relationships in your life and your family. Do not parrot Satan's lie that God cannot do this and God cannot do that. He said that you and I can do all things through Christ who strengthens us (Phil. 4:13).

Our God is bigger than any physical house. He is not limited; rather, He is *El Shaddai*, the God that is more than enough. We must believe this, and we must tell it to the people in the community. They should know that God is not limited in our churches. Do the people who come know that we will pray for them? When people know there is a church that does not put limits on God, they will flock to that church and stick to it like gravy on rice.

What do people in your city say about your church? Do they observe, "You know what? They believe in miracles; they believe in healing. There is no limit to what God can do!" That is what the church's reputation ought to be.

Why should we have to ask the world for new medication for our ailments? There is nothing wrong with receiving medical help, but the church has to rise to the constitutional truth that God cannot be limited. We are talking about the house of God here. We must declare in word and practice the truth that God is not limited in the church. All things are possible to those who believe (Mark 9:23). Oh, I like this; it is exciting!

That thine eyes may be open upon this house day and night, upon the place whereof thou hast said that thou wouldest put thy name there; to hearken unto the prayer which thy servant prayeth toward this place.

—2 CHRONICLES 6:20

DISPLAYING
THE NAME OF GOD

———◆·◆·◆———

The identity of the church, instead of
being based on the pastor or anything
of human origin, should be found in
God's name.

This verse says that the house of God is a place where the name of God is displayed. The church is to show forth the names of God. Just as we identify one another with a name, people should be able to come and identify that God is *Jehovah Shalom*, the Lord God of peace. He is *Jehovah Jireh*, the Lord God, my provider. He is *Jehovah Tsidkenu*, the Lord God, my victory. He is *El Shaddai*, the God that is more than enough. He is the I AM, the Lamb of God.

As heirs and joint heirs with Christ, we can identify with these names of God. However, too many people do not know the names of God. They are going the house of God and do not have the slightest clue about who God is. They do not know that He is the God who is more than enough. They do not know that He is the God of peace, the God of victory. Oh yes! He is the God who supplies.

The church must identify with the names of God. I preach in churches all over America, and every one of them is different. Some are fired up, and others are stiff and out of touch with God. The climate in churches is a gumbo, and, from a Cajun aspect a gumbo is a little bit of everything. I cannot imagine what God thinks.

One time I went to a church where everyone wanted to lay hands on me. I had to warn them, "Don't lay hands on me. Don't touch me at all because I don't know what you want to impart or depart." They wanted to give me a word, and I do not have a problem with words. I believe in the gifts of the Spirit. But when everyone in the place wanted to prophesy, I questioned it.

My identification, Mark Duplantis, doesn't mean anything. What impacts the lives of people is that I declare the names of God and offer a message of peace and hope. I can boldly declare the message that God is going to take care of you. He is going to heal you and do great and mighty things. He is going to show Himself strong on your behalf. That is what people need. We do not need a Duplantis name; we need God's name.

The identity of the church, instead of being based on the pastor or anything of human origin, should be found in God's name. When people drive by, they should recognize it as a place that is excelling and growing. They should know it as a place they can go to receive prayer for healing and meet with people who believe in miracles.

Yes, some may say, "Oh, I don't believe in healing." Well if they get cancer, they will. When the doctors and everyone else gives up on their recovery, they will change their theology. Others may reason, "Oh, I don't believe in prosperity." Well, when they are financially broke and are losing everything, they will not condemn those who believe that God will supply all our needs, wants, and desires. Isn't this good news? It is God's plan to make His church a house that displays the names of God.

Hearken therefore unto the supplications of thy servant, and of thy people Israel, which they shall make toward this place: hear thou from thy dwelling place, even from heaven; and when thou hearest, forgive.

—2 Chronicles 6:21

FORGIVENESS
AND RIGHTEOUSNESS

*The house of God is to be a place of
reconciliation for those who need to be
restored to relationship with Him.*

Solomon's dedication prayer asks God to make
His house a place of forgiveness. Even though
some of us do not want to forgive others, this is
what God wants to manifest in the church.

Now, I have had people do me wrong. Has
that happened to you since you have been saved?
Have you ever had a bad thought against people
who have done you wrong? We must forgive. God's
house must display that people who have wronged
others or stolen from them can come and find forgiveness. Whatever they did, we cannot allow cor-
rupt communication to come out of our mouths,
but we must speak that which will build them up
(Eph. 4:25–29).

I would be dishonest if I did not acknowledge that I do not want to forgive some people. I want to be God about five seconds and settle things my way. I know I am not the only one who has ever thought that way, but it is not right. I must minister forgiveness if I am going to identify with the constitution of the house of God. I must walk in forgiveness.

We often have a problem with forgiveness because we have not learned how to forgive ourselves of past deeds. You see, the enemy wants to use our past to condemn us. He says, "Aw, man, you've been married 49 times; you were a prostitute, a junkie, a drug addict, and you're still having a tough time with some stuff." He uses past sins and failures against us and after a while condemnation sets in, causing us to feel like a dirty, filthy rat.

Jesus says that if we learn to forgive, we will fly out of the washing machine, hit the dryer, and come out with a fragrance. Yes, we will come out with fragrance, a sweet smelling fragrance that is acceptable in the very nostrils of God. This is what God wants for the church, the house of God. We must forgive others, no matter what they have done to us.

We have to love others, but we do not have to like everything about them. Do you see the difference? I have to love you—and I am going to love you—but that does not mean I have to like you. My wife does not like everything I do, but she loves me. I do things that she does not like, but she still chooses to love me. We have dislikes, but love keeps us together.

If you have done me wrong, I can forgive you. The church is to be a house of forgiveness. When we minister forgiveness, we are set free. We are released from bondage. Isn't that good?

A HOUSE OF
RIGHTEOUS JUDGMENT

> If a man sin against his neighbor, and an oath be laid upon him to make him swear, and the oath come before thine altar in this house; Then hear thou from heaven, and do, and judge thy servants, by requiting the wicked, by recompensing his way upon his own head; and by justifying the righteous, by giving him according to his righteousness.
>
> —2 CHRONICLES 6:22–23

We must have righteous judgement in the house of God so we do not have laws trying to govern according to man's ways instead of God's ways. If we followed God's constitution we would not have all the immoral acts like abortion, same-sex marriages, or courts trying to decide our faith.

The house of God is to be a place where unity is protected. Even though there may be disagreement in the house of God, we can agree to disagree and preserve unity (Amos 3:3; Matt. 18:19). We need to understand this because it is going to help us. We are going to have disagreements at home—between husband and wife—about the way things are run.

Or we might disagree with the pastor or with another person in the church.

Oh, how we need protection for unity! We are much too open to sources of division. I know what it is like when something tries to crawl into my spirit and create disagreement that could sever my relationship with another person. But we can come to the house of God where God's presence is, and He shows mercy and grace and forgiveness. In God's house, we can walk in the unity of the Spirit. How can any two walk together except they be in agreement? God says His church, the house of God, is to protect unity.

A House of Reconciliation

> And if thy people of Israel be put to the worse before the enemy, because they have sinned against thee; and shall return and confess thy name, and pray and make supplication before thee in this house; Then hear thou from the heavens, and forgive the sin of thy people Israel, and bring them again unto the land which thou gavest to them and to their fathers.
>
> —2 Chronicles 6:24–25

These verses speak of reconciliation. The house of God is to be a place of reconciliation for those who need to be restored to relationship with Him. God demonstrated this through His Son Jesus, and we have been reconciled to Him. We must also extend this gracious ministry when people come and say, "You know, I said some wrong things when I left. But I am returning because you show reconciliation here."

Oh, how necessary it is that we understand this! It is so vital and meaningful. The church is to be a place of reconciliation, not just in individual relationships, but on a corporate level. When this is true, people who have left the church can be reconciled to God and us because we welcome them back. However, they cannot come back the same way they left. Until they deal with the root of sin, they will keep producing bad fruit.

Yes, the church should be a place of reconciliation; it is what every church should display.

When the heaven is shut up, and there is no rain, because they have sinned against thee; yet if they pray toward this place, and confess thy name, and turn from their sin, when thou dost afflict them; Then hear thou from heaven, and forgive the sin of thy servants, and of thy people Israel, when thou has taught them the good way, wherein they should walk; and send rain upon thy land, which thou hast given unto thy people for an inheritance.

—2 Chronicles 6:26–27

LIVING UNDER
SHOWERS OF BLESSINGS

—◆·❖·◆—

*Solomon shows that the house of
God is to be a place of healing for the
body and the soul.*

Every church should be a place with showers of
blessing. In the natural realm, we come out clean
and feel refreshed after a shower. But after a while, we
start to stink again and no longer feel good. What do
we do? We go back and take another shower. What
should we do when the blessings stop flowing in the
house of God? Repent—turn away from sin—and
let the showers start again.

We do not have to go way back and pay our sin
debt. No, we just repent and go on. People come to
me and say, "Well, I haven't tithed in five years. If I
go by what the Bible says, I sure have a whole lot to
pay back to God."

"You're right," I tell them. "But if you repent and

start tithing from this moment on, you are forgiven. If you don't, God will hold you accountable for the thousands and thousands of dollars you owe, for wearing stolen clothes, and for driving stolen cars."

Do you understand what I am saying? A house of God must be a place where there are showers of blessing. When people drive by or walk in, they should say, "Surely God rains upon this house." When the showers stop we must repent. And when we do, the showers return.

A House of Healing

If there be dearth [famine] in the land, if there be pestilence, if there be blasting [blight] or mildew, locusts or caterpillars; if their enemies besiege them in the cities of their land; whatsoever sore or whatsoever sickness there be: Then what prayer or what supplication soever shall be made of any man, or of all thy people Israel when every one shall know his own sore and his own grief, and shall spread forth his hands in this house: Then hear thou from heaven thy dwelling place, and forgive, and render unto every man according unto all his ways, whose heart thou knowest; (for thou only knowest the hearts of the children of men:) That they may fear thee, to walk in thy ways, so long as they live in the land which thou gavest unto our fathers.

—2 Chronicles 6:28–31

Solomon shows that the house of God is to be a place of healing for the body and the soul. Some of us do not need physical healing, but we need healing for the soul—the mind, will, and emotions. When people speak of the church, they should be able to say, "Yes, I guarantee that you will receive healing there. It's the house of God, and they live by the constitution, which provides for healing of the body, the spirit, and the soul."

We can come to the church and receive healing for mental and emotional needs. Oh, what good news! We renew our minds by listening to the Word of God instead of all the garbage in the world. It is important that we spend time with people who have faith and speak what the Word says, not what someone else thinks.

This reminds me of a story about an acrobat who was by a waterfall. A crowd was there, and he looked at them and asked, "How many of you have faith that I can walk on this tightrope across the waterfall?"

The people cheered him on and shouted, "Yeah, you can do it!"

He walked on the tightrope over the waterfall, and the crowd cheered because he made it across. In response, he asked them another question, "How many of you believe that I can walk blindfolded on this tightrope and cross the waterfall?"

Once again they cried, "We have faith. We know you can do it!"

37

And he did it. He was blindfolded and walked on the tightrope to the other side of the waterfall. Of course, the crowd cheered because he had made it.

Now he asked them a third question, "How many of you have faith that I can walk blindfolded on this tightrope and push a wheelbarrow over the waterfall?"

"Oh, yeah," the people cried once more. "We know you can do it. You've done it twice already. Surely you can do it!"

So, he crossed the waterfall blindfolded, pushing a wheelbarrow. When he reached the other side, he spoke to the crowd. "You have expressed faith that I can walk blindfolded on this tightrope and push a wheelbarrow cross the waterfall. Now, how many of you believe that I can walk blindfolded on this tight rope and push a person in a wheelbarrow to the other side of the waterfall?"

"Oh, yeah, you can do it!" the people cheered.

"May I have a volunteer?" he asked.

How much faith do you have? Is it based on God's Word or only on the things other people say or think? Do you truly believe God in the pressure-filled tightrope situations of life? The house of God is to be a place where people, by faith, receive healing of the body and the soul.

Moreover concerning the stranger, which is not of thy people Israel [the ones who are not of our church background], but is come from a far country for thy great name's sake, and thy mighty hand, and thy stretched out arm; if they come and pray in this house; Then hear thou from the heavens, even from thy dwelling place, and do according to all that the stranger calleth to thee for; that all people of the earth may know by name, and fear thee, as doth thy people Israel, and may know that this house which I have built is called by thy name.

—2 Chronicles 6:32–33

ACTIVE IN
KINGDOM MINISTRY

*Solomon shows that the house of
God is to be a place of healing for the
body and the soul.*

I n these verses Solomon is praying prophetically
about the salvation and evangelism of the gen-
tiles hundreds of years before Jesus came. He is saying that the house of God is for all, long before the
apostle Paul came upon the scene or Peter ever had
the revelation about the uncircumcised.

Salvation and evangelism are present in the
house of God—the church. People will come to
the church from the north, the south, the east, and
the west to receive the salvation God has provided
through faith in Jesus Christ. People who are not
homegrown are going to come into our communi-
ties, and it is important that we do not reject them
because they are not from our geographical area or

our church background.

God wants the church to be a place where all people can feel welcome and receive salvation, no matter what they have done in their lives. They need to know that the love of God is present in the church. After we dedicate the house of God, we have to be careful that we do not forget about it and push our agenda instead of God's agenda. We must guard against throwing out God's constitution and replacing it with our own laws.

A HOUSE AT WAR WITH THE ENEMY

> If thy people go out to war against their enemies by the way that thou shall send them, and they pray unto thee toward this city which thou has chosen, and the house which I have built for thy name; Then hear thou from the heavens their prayer and their supplication, and maintain their cause.
>
> —2 CHRONICLES 6:34–35

This is a prayer of spiritual warfare, that God will maintain the cause of His people. Why? Simply put, we are at war with the enemy.

I wonder if God would vote for you if you were running for public office. If God was going to vote, the first thing He would want to know is your platform. He would want to know about your political experience and your ability to lead. And He would check out your war on terror. Do you think He would vote for you if you could not show Him that you are engaging in warfare?

The house of God—the church—is to be involved in spiritual warfare. As the apostle Paul says in Ephesians 6:12, we are fighting against a very real spiritual enemy. It is a truth that calls us to be vigilant and prepared.

If they sin against thee, (for there is no man which sinneth not,) and thou be angry with them, and deliver them over before their enemies, and they carry them away captives unto a land far off or near; Yet if they bethink themselves in the land whither they are carried captive, and turn and pray unto thee in the land of their captivity, saying, We have sinned, we have done amiss, and have dealt wickedly; If they return to thee with all their heart and with all their soul in the land of their captivity, whither they have carried them captives, and pray toward their land, which thou gavest unto their fathers, and toward the city which thou hast chosen, and toward the house which I have built for thy name: Then hear thou from the heavens, even from thy dwelling place, their prayer and their supplications, and maintain their cause, and forgive thy people which have sinned against thee.

—2 CHRONICLES 6:36–39

REVIVAL
AND HABITATION

*When we give God His
place of habitation, we have Him
all the time.*

I really love this! The house of God is a place of revival. Verse 38 speaks about revival on three levels: national (the land), citywide (the city), and in the church (the house of God). The church is to be praying for a revival in all these parts of society.

Stop and think about that. Too many Christians live a life of survival when they need revival. We have been watching the *Survivor* series so long that we do not understand what revival is all about. Before we are ever really going to see revival, we have to be "re-Bibled." We are to pray for revival in our land, our cities, and our churches. Yes, that is what we are to do.

Most of us hardly pray for the house—the local church—and God calls us to pray for the land and the city too. If we do not like what we see in our city, we need to pray for God to change it. That is the answer. The house of God is a place where revival begins, and it can start in any church in any location. We do not have to be in Pensacola, Florida, or Toronto, Ontario. No, we just have to be in a house of God.

Our God does not love the church in Pensacola or Toronto more than the church in any other city. He is just looking for a house where the people know how to pray for the land, the city, and the local church. And He promises that when we do, revival is coming to the house of God. This excites me. I cannot wait until the day when I am invited to a church that fulfills everything Solomon describes in 2 Chronicles 6.[1] I think I will rapture and go to heaven!

THE HOUSE OF GOD'S HABITATION

Now, my God, let, I beseech thee, thine eyes be open, and let thy ears be attent unto the prayer that is made in this place. Now therefore arise, O LORD God, unto thy resting place, thou, and the ark of thy strength: let thy priests, O LORD God, be clothed with salvation, and let thy saints rejoice in goodness. O LORD God, turn not away the face of thine anointed: remember the mercies of David thy servant.

—2 CHRONICLES 6:40–42

The house of God is the place of His habitation, not merely His visitation. Too many of us want God to show up in a temporary visitation when we should allow Him to have habitation. We are waiting for some glory cloud to appear. Now I like a glory cloud every now and then, but too many of us have a mental picture of God coming on a visitation instead taking His place of habitation.

I want God to be in the house every time I come through the doors. I want to see Him every time my eyes are open. I want His presence wherever I am walking or talking. In everything I do, I want God to make His habitation inside of me. But we, in our mentality, hope that God will visit our meetings. We wonder if He is going to show up. Well, He is at every meeting when we, His people, gather in Christ's name. He has made a habitation inside of us; the third Person of the Godhead lives and resides in us. Yes, we are the house of God.

We need to realize that God wants habitation. When we give God His place of habitation, we have Him all the time. We experience miracles and healing all the time, and we receive forgiveness all the time. We enjoy all the blessings of the constitution of the house of God all the time.

I am tired of getting a little goose bump on my goose bump. I am tired of just getting a little twitch every now and then. No, I want to wake up in His presence and go to sleep in His presence. I want to travel on the highway and not be vexed with the way people drive.

Yes, I want God to have a habitation in me. The benefits are multiple. When I speak to Him, He says, "Yes, Mark." When I ask for His provision, He says, "What do you need? I already know what you have need of, before you even ask, but I love to hear it." Since He has habitation in me, I do not have to try to bring Him down from heaven. He is already here.

I do not need visitation; I need habitation. However, it seems that some are only looking for a little visit. *Oh God I'm short on money this month, please help me pay my mortgage.* But after He does that, they do not even talk to Him the rest of the month. And after a while, they have to invite Him for another visit.

But when God makes His habitation in us, He moves in. He is not going anywhere. You see, the Holy Spirit is committed to you and me, even if we die physically and go the way of the grave.

Do you know what the Holy Spirit, who lives in the Christian, does when that person dies? Does He go back to heaven? No! Guess where He is? I do not care if a Christian is buried in the middle of a cotton field in an unmarked grave. I do not care if an interstate highway is built over his grave. The Holy Spirit is still there, waiting for the voice of God, ready to raise his dead body so he can go to be with Jesus. When God makes His habitation in us, we are not forgotten.

*For unto us a child is born, unto us a son
is given: and the government shall be upon
his shoulder: and his name shall be called
Wonderful, Counsellor, The mighty God,
The everlasting Father, The Prince of Peace.*
—ISAIAH 9:6

THE CONSTITUTION
IS SEALED

*The Scriptures say that God's house is
going to be a place of purity, prayer,
power, and praise.*

God accepted everything Solomon prayed for
in 2 Chronicles 6:12–42. He did not oppose
one thing that Solomon prayed. Isn't that good?
And these petitions of Solomon form the constitution of the house of God. Solomon covered it all.
God made sure that the constitution of His house
was complete and without error. There is no loop-
hole in it and no need for amendments.

More than nine hundred years later Jesus came
on the scene and walked into another temple. Solomon's temple had been destroyed when the Babylo-
nians ravaged Jerusalem in 586 B.C. After the exiled
Jews returned from Babylon to Jerusalem, they
completed a second temple in 516 B.C. It fell into

disrepair, and Herod the Great began restoring it about 20 B.C.

This was the temple Jesus visited in Matthew 21. He did not go there to dedicate it. He already knew what Solomon had prayed, and His Father had accepted it as the constitution. But when Jesus went into the temple, He sealed the deal. In other words, He reinforced all that Solomon had prayed and all that His Father had accepted. He condensed it and declared what the house of God is going to be. Let's look at what He said, both in deed and word.

A House of Purity

> And Jesus went into the temple of God, and cast out all them that sold and bought in the temple, and overthrew the tables of the moneychangers, and the seats of them that sold doves.
>
> —Matthew 21:12

Jesus did not come to establish a constitution but to operate as government. State and local government are responsible to point us back to the constitution. Here Jesus as government is pointing them to the constitution, which His Father had already established through Solomon concerning the temple or house of God. Today we operate as government (ambassadors) for Christ.

When Jesus went into the temple, He found greedy businessmen violating the anointing in the temple. They were selling crippled pigeons that were not even worthy of sacrifice. Jesus cast them out, with all their unrighteous practices. His actions affirmed and supported what Solomon had said in his prayer of dedication for the temple. He showed that the house of God was going to be a house of purity, in agreement with Solomon's prayer.

The church is also going to be a place of purity. If we want to live a corrupted life we cannot stay. But if we want purity this is the place to come. Instead of accepting the immorality and perversion that is so rampant today, the church must listen to Jesus. He comes and says that the temple is going to be a house of purity.

A House of Prayer, Power, and Praise

> And He said unto them, It is written, My house shall be called the house of prayer; but ye have made it a den of thieves. And the blind and the lame came to him in the temple; and he healed them. And when the chief priests and scribes saw the wonderful things that he did, and the children crying in the temple, and saying, Hosanna to the son of David; they were sore displeased.
>
> —Matthew 21:13–15

Jesus said that the temple was going to be not only a house of purity, but also a house of prayer. This was just as Solomon had prayed. When the blind and the lame came to Him in the temple, Jesus healed them. First, the house of God is a place of purity. Then it becomes a house of prayer and a house of power. This is what God wants the church to be.

The atmosphere in the temple changed when Jesus started healing the sick. Children cried out with praise to Him. Jesus enacted all that Solomon prayed for the temple, and it became a place of purity, prayer, power—and praise.

This is the constitution of the house of God. Our churches must have structure, the basic laws of God's covenant. Just as the Wal-Marts, the Home Depots, and other chain stores follow the plans established by their corporate leadership, each church must implement God's government. We must follow God's ways instead of man's ways. And then we will have much more than a visitation of God. We will enjoy the habitation of God.

The Scriptures say that God's house is going to be a place of purity, prayer, power, and praise. The church is to reflect all these things, in its meetings as a body and in its witness to the community. If we follow the constitution He has given in His Word, it is guaranteed that we will be a house of reconciliation for a world that desperately needs salvation.

To Contact the Author

Web site: www.MarkDuplantis.com
E-mail: markduplantis@charter.net